SUN DESIGNS

D0478346

93 New Ideas for Leisure Time Enjoyment

Ekman

Gazebos and Other Garden Structures

Authors.......................Janet A. Strombeck
Richard H. Strombeck
Illustrated by......................Marlene Ekman
Robert Petersen
Garden Structure Designs...........Marlene Ekman
James Klopp
Steven Sharpe
Strombrellas Designed by...........Marlene Ekman

Birdfeeders & Houses Designed by........James Klopp
Graphic & Art Direction............Marlene Ekman
Robert Petersen
Edited by...........................Ann Tomasic
Published by.........................Sun Designs
P.O. Box 206
Delafield, WI 53018
Telephone: 414-567-4255

Copyright ©1983 by Rexstrom Co., Inc. All rights reserved. No part of this publication may be reproduced or used in any form or by any means, stored in a retrieval system or transmitted in any form or by any means, electronic, mechanical, photographic, recording, or otherwise, without the prior written permission of the Publisher.
Printed in the U.S.A.

ISBN 0-912355-00-X

FORWORD

My interest in gazebos began five years ago when I and my husband made a decision to build one in our lawn and garden area. Like most projects, the decision was the easiest part. Our search for gazebo plans began very confidently at a local bookstore, and from there to a larger bookstore, and from there to a larger bookstore, and then libraries, lumber yards, plywood companies, mail order plan services, and hundreds of magazines, all without success. We came to the realization that if we were going to have a gazebo, we would have to find someone to design one with complete working drawings.

Almost simultaneously, we met a recently graduated architect with whom we discussed our project. With his imagination, a number of preliminary design ideas began to develop.

As we showed these designs to our friends, neighbors, and people in our office, we found many of them requesting copies of the gazebo plans for their own use. It was at this time that we decided to expand the preliminary designs we already had to a total of twenty-three and publish them.

The book of twenty-three was successful and in response to many requests, two years later we expanded the twenty-three designs to thirty-four and it, too, was successful. We are very pleased with your response to these books.

Since publishing our first Gazebo Study Plan Book three years ago, we have received many requests from all over America for special gazebo designs, as well as specialty lawn and garden shelters. We liked the resulting designs so well that we decided to make a third revision of our gazebo book. We fully intend this to be the last revision as we wish to shift our efforts toward other subject matter.

This book like the original one, is an attempt to build a bridge between better personalized design and economical design costs for people like ourselves who enjoy their home, its outdoor areas and wish to add to it the joys a gazebo can provide.

As we appear to be the best source for gazebo plans, we have tried to meet your needs and publish the most requested "special" design features along with many of the earlier thirty-four designs. We have, in this book, a greater variety of sizes and roof designs since we found that many people start with a very definite space requirement in which to build. Also included are arbor designs and a feature we think is different and exciting—strombrellas. They are small decorative structures shading a lawn activity area such as a swing, sand box, picnic table, or anything else your imagination can picture. We hope you like them as much as we do.

To make this a more complete book for your lawn or garden area we have also included a few bird feeders and bird houses. What a pleasure it is to have them around your home.

Many people have written us that they had a hard time making a decision from the previous thirty-four designs. We realize we have added to this problem, but we hope that everyone can find **something** to please them in this book.

We have labored to serve this end and hope you like the results.

INTRODUCTION

A gazebo is like a sun porch in the middle of your lawn or garden. It can be a simple roof supported on four plain columns or an elaborate, stained glass, paneled, enclosed structure. Modern uses for gazebos include a place for a quiet luncheon, brunch or tea, a private shady place to read or talk, a focal point for parties, weddings and showers or as a bandstand or hot tub enclosure. In fact, we have gotten many pictures and letters confirming most of these uses. These pictures all look so beautiful!

Our gazebo designs have many interchanging features so that your SUN DESIGN gazebo can be different from anyone else's. Let your imagination run and design your own gazebo or select one as shown. The many railings, fascia and brackets found in the back of the book can usually be interchanged with almost any design to suit your personal taste. We have added quite a few to this book.

So, whether you prefer Victorian, Oriental, Modern or Traditional there is one to make your dream gazebo exactly what it should be—all your own.

PLANS

Each design has been professionally prepared with easy to understand, completely detailed construction drawings showing foundation and floor plans, construction section, elevation, special connection details, railing and finial details along with full size decorative bracket and fascia details for use as templates.

Included along with each set of plans is an itemized materials list "guide". Types, sizes and amounts are listed, along with a short glossary of terms and abbreviations used on the plans to assist the non-carpenter builder. Materials specified are common to most local lumber yards and hardware stores; railings, fascia and brackets can usually be made by a millwork shop or woodturner, or possibly a vocational school.

We do not sell any finished wood products, only the plans.

If you prefer a different railing, bracket or fascia over that shown on your chosen plan, choose one from the alternates **shown** only.

We have given you many plans to choose from, so we hope you find something **you** like. Remember, a gazebo is an affair of the heart.

Good luck and enjoy your gazebo.

Janet A. Strombeck

THE STORY OF THE GAZEBOS

Man has sought to cultivate and adorn his garden since Adam and Eve left the Garden of Eden. Gazebos are truly as old as the art of gardening itself. These small garden structures are often called summerhouses, screen houses, belvederes, pavilions, kiosks, bowers, arbors, pergolas, gloriettas, teahouses, temples, grottos, and pagodas to name a few. By whatever name they are called today, they are commonly used as a center for entertaining, special events and a personal retreat for physical and spiritual regeneration.

As might be expected, kings, queens and nobles were the first to have gazebos erected in their gardens. Five thousand years ago they were a common feature in Egyptian gardens. In approximately 1400 B.C., during the reign of King Amenhotep III, a most complete plan of a villa and its surrounding ground showing a garden plan, complete with planting order and location of two small garden pavilions, each overlooking a pool, was discovered in a Theban tomb. A painted scene found in another tomb of the same period contains a detail of a large garden in which a small garden house and a large pond are depicted. Many Egyptian nobles believed in a life hereafter and planned their tombs long before old age. If they had enjoyed their garden when alive and wanted to take it with them into their next life they, by custom, would have their garden depicted in a mural on their tomb.

Ancient Rome and Pompeii also had their summerhouses. In the year 62 A.D. Pliny the Younger describes two residences he owned in a letter to a friend. One of them, called Tusci, was in the foothills of the Appennines and contained a "garden house shaded by plane trees." When he built this celebrated villa in Como, he gave it two towers and, as an early writer noted, "they could be used neither for defense in such a place, nor for smoking rooms at such an early period, we can only suppose them to have been erected to serve as gazebos whence he could gaze into the grounds of his neighbor and watch their incomings and outgoings."

The more crowded Rome became, the more vacation villas were built in the country and along the shores of the Mediterranean. Pompeii and Herculaneum flourished and from what has been reconstructed it appears to have been an aristocratic place of fine villas with summerhouses, pergolas and colonnades on terraces facing the sea.

With the decline of the Roman Empire during the Dark Ages and the early part of the Middle Ages, the interest in garden houses declined and records of their existence are poor or do not exist in Europe.

But in the East, at this same period, garden houses were flourishing. The Koran states that the Day of Judgment will take place "in gardens of Pleasure" and, Moslems built beautiful gardens and summerhouses.

In Persia, a typical garden was laid out in four sections with water channels dividing the sections. Where the water channels intersected, there was usually either a pool or a small hill with a pavilion on it. Fantastic descriptions of Persian gardens in the tenth century are recorded. They tell of precious metals decorating marble columns, of seats of gold in the garden summerhouses and magnificent views. The designs of garden shelters varied widely. Some were merely colorful tents or awnings with rugs placed beneath to sit on, while others were built with beautiful mosaic tile, or two-storied pavilions on railed platforms with miniature towers on the roof. Others were built across pools so that cold water flowing under the marble floors would keep them cool.

Fortunately this rich Persian heritage did not come to an end when the Mongolian and Tartar invasion came in the 13th century. Baber, the first Mogul Emperor actually created many more gardens, ten alone in Kabul, now part of Afghanistan. These pleasure gardens of the Moguls often contained marble garden houses for banquets, court receptions, and for relaxing from battles. Many were even used as tombs for the owners.

It was during the Sung Period (960-1280) in China, a time of enlightenment, that its gardens and summerhouses reached a high degree of development. It would be more than two centuries later before the Western World would receive word from Marco Polo of the beautifully tiled garden houses or simple rustic ones as diverse as the views they commanded.

The Japanese summerhouse and teahouses are believed to be imports from China. They were built to serve as resting places where one could enjoy solitude or the beauty of the garden. The teahouse is an extension of the tea garden and is planned to be conducive to meditation and be in harmony with the spirit of the Tea Ceremony, the purpose of which is to impress upon the mind the virtues of modesty, politeness, restraint, and sensibility. They are generally located in a secluded spot and there may be more than one in a garden, each a different design style.

As the western world began to emerge from the middle ages into the Rennaissance period, ornate garden houses returned in popularity and no proper garden was without a summerhouse of some kind and a few were extravagant to the point of scandal. Garden shelters became common in monastery gardens where they functioned as shrines used for prayer or just as decorative places where the soul could find nourishment.

A famous 13th century Italian writer, Crescentius, advised his readers about the importance of little summerhouses and many followed his advice. A little stone summerhouse on Pincian Hill with a beautiful view of Rome was originally built by the famous and powerful Medici family and was later owned and enjoyed by cardinals, grand dukes, and, eventually, by Napoleon.

France had many garden houses. Four of them were built at the Louvre in the 14th century and influenced building in many other countries. In 1784, Marie Antoinette gave a splendid reception at her favorite hideaway Le Petite Trianon situated in a faraway corner of the park at Versailles. Swedish King Gustave III was "quite impressed" with the exquisite little pavilion there and returned to Stockholm with plans for a Turkish Pavilion to be built by the Royal Summer Residence at Haga.

Little garden houses became very popular in England in the 15th century after being introduced from France. They, too, were placed on little grassy knolls or on the corners of garden walls offering vantage points to the garden or upon the wilder landscape outside the garden. Substantial remains of some of these can be found today.

In the Kings New Garden, built by Henry VIII, there was an elegant three-story summerhouse constructed with much glass and topped with a lead cupola which in turn was fitted with a "beeste" and weather vane.

Summerhouses were also used as the central feature of mazes made with shrubbery which were so high that people could get lost in them. But generally they were used in the Elizabethan garden for outdoor entertaining and relaxation, often similar in design and materials to the main house. A writer of that time recommended the summerhouse to be placed remote from "the frequent disturbances of your family and acquaintances." While another said its best purpose was for sorting and drying garden bulbs.

In the late 1700's, Chinese design swept England and Europe and Chinese-style summerhouses were the rage in Anglo-Chinese gardens. It wasn't until the mid-1700's that the Germans became heavily involved in garden shelter. By the time Queen Victoria took the throne, romanticists, influenced by Sir Walter Scott novels, emphasized Gothic design in summerhouses and arbors. Equally popular were the rustic garden houses fashioned from tree roots and branches.

Summerhouses were not common in early America as the struggle for survival left little time for gazebos, but the ideas and tradition these immigrants brought with them would influence a later generation.

In a book published in 1705, Robert Beverly, brother-in-law of William Byrd II of Virginia wrote "Colonel Byrd, in his garden which is the finest in that county, has a summerhouse set round with Indian Honey Suckle . . . the inconvenience of heat is made easier by cool shades, by open airy rooms, summerhouses, arbors and grottos."

Thomas Jefferson, James Madison and George Washington all had an interest in gazebos. While Thomas Jefferson did not build one, he had written about them and reportedly designed one for James Madison. George Washington had a small octagonal summerhouse at Mount Vernon.

One could not say gazebos were popular in America. By and large, we were still a country of rich and poor with only a few garden shelters. They were either extravagant or nothing.

It was not until the middle 1800's and 1900 that gazebos became extremely popular in America and reached their high point in American architectural ornamentation. This is understandable with the rise of a new, relatively prosperous middle class anxious to show and enjoy the fruits of their labor; a status symbol showing that they had "made it". Besides it is a timeless place to rest and an old-fashioned place of peace and pleasure. But in early 1900, gazebos lost popularity, in part, because many houses built after that date had fine porches. By 1930, gazebos began to return even among houses with fine screen porches. I think it became apparent that a gazebo, with its appealing smallness, could provide a sense of intimate privacy that a porch attached to a house, with its attendant hustle and bustle, could not provide.

Gazebos continued increasing in popularity and at the same time became simpler in construction with solid or open roof and sidewall until the 1940s. Then, the patio arrived on the scene and more recently the deck. A porch without a roof. What an invention!

But people have found the gazebo again. There is no question about the strong resurgence of interest for the gazebo in the 1980s. Literally, thousands are being built all over America.

A gazebo is truly the perfect prescription for us now. It is the antithesis of the jet age. It is not dedicated to speed or busy-ness or schedules, but a place of seclusion, a momentary retreat from todays space age, a place to sneak a nap or day dream, a place to have a good warming drink in your fall sweater.

Gazebos are very adaptable to the whims of the designer, as well as locally available materials. Their form can also vary with local architecture and are not easily typed. They can be ornate or simple, round or square, octagon or rectangle, classic or rustic, colonnaded or closed, peaked or flat. It doesn't really matter as long as it's becoming.

Its location is equally flexible. But gazebos deserve a place of honor in the landscape and seem most inviting when removed from outdoor activities by a distance.

There is no better way to end a terrace or long walk than with a gazebo. In small yards the gazebo may be nestled against a wall and screened from other activities by a wooden lattice, tastefully planted with climbing roses or clematis, and thinned to let the light filter in to encourage the growth of other plants within the framework.

It has justifiably been said of American gardens that though they are pretty to look at, they have not enough places where one may sit in comfort and enjoy them.

Gazebos serve as a fitting resting place where one may enjoy the solitude and beauty of nature. They are a place of peace and rest where the soul can find nourishment, a place to browse in a book or write or sketch. They can be placed for intimate conversation or a leisurely lunch with a special friend, a place away from household distractions and telephones and callers, a monument to the contemplative life and nostalgic romance of the past and, especially, a place for young **and** old lovers (like you and me).

GAZEBOS

STRATFORD

Size: Thirteen feet point to point.
Height: Sixteen feet, four inches. See floor plan No. 9.

Size: Eight feet, four inches by eight feet, four inches.
Height: Sixteen feet, four inches. See floor plan No. 14.

MEADOWVIEW

Size: Sixteen feet by sixteen feet.
Height: Fourteen feet, four inches. See floor plan No. 36.

Size: Fifteen feet point to point.
Height: Sixteen feet. See floor plan No. 4.

WEXFORD

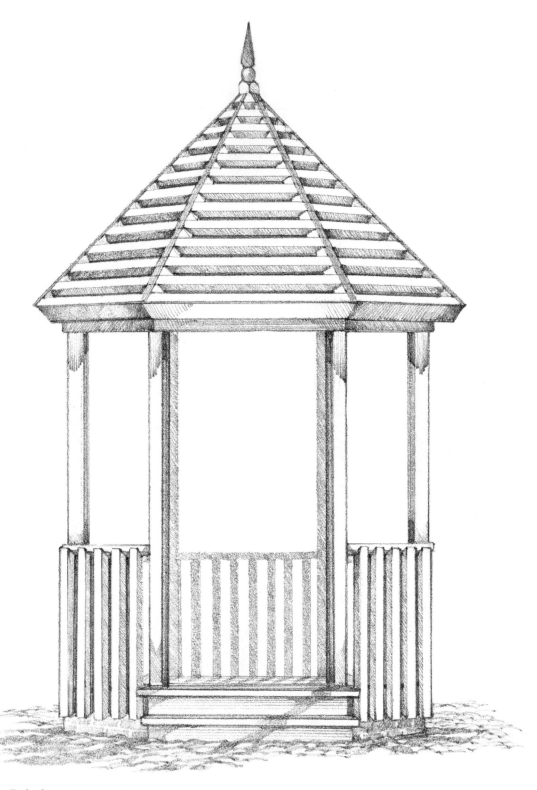

Size: Eight feet point to point.
Height: Fifteen feet, two inches. See floor plan No. 2.

Size: Ten feet by ten feet.
Height: Sixteen feet, eight inches. See floor plan No. 18.

CHALET

Size: Twelve feet by sixteen feet.
Height: Thirteen feet. See floor plan 25.

Size: Twelve feet point to point.
Height: Twenty-three feet, nine inches. See floor plan No. 5.

LIGHTHOUSE

Size: Ten feet by ten feet.
Height: Fourteen feet, eight inches. See floor plan No. 19.

Size: Nine feet, two inches point to point.
Height: Fourteen feet, nine inches. See floor plan No. 1.

FAIRWOOD

Size: Thirteen feet point to point.
Height: Thirteen feet, eight inches. See floor plan No. 9.
Has center support & post.

Size: Thirteen feet point to point.
Height: Twelve feet, six inches. See floor plan No. 9.

ROANOKE

Size: Six feet by twelve feet.
Height: Twelve feet. See floor plan No. 16.

Size: Fourteen feet by fourteen feet.
Height: Seventeen feet, eight inches. See floor plan No. 31.

CUPOLA

Size: Nine feet by nine feet.
Height: Sixteen feet. See floor plan No. 15.

Size: Seventeen feet, eight inches.
Height: Fourteen feet, eight inches. See floor plan No. 6.

VALDEZ

Size: Nine feet, two inches point to point.
Height: Fifteen feet. See floor plan No. 1.

CAROUSELLE

Size: Thirteen feet point to point.
Height: Eighteen feet, nine inches.
See floor plan No. 9.

COLONNADE

Size: Thirteen feet point to point.
Height: Fourteen feet, six inches. See floor plan No. 8.

Size: Ten feet by ten feet.
Height: Sixteen feet, four inches. See floor plan No. 20.

AVALON

Size: Fifteen feet point to point.
Height: Nineteen feet. See floor plan No. 4.

Size: Thirteen feet point to point.
Height: Twenty feet, four inches. See floor plan No. 9.

TRAVELER

Size: Seven feet, four inches.
Height: Eleven feet. See floor plan No. 3.
Knock—down Model

Size: Twelve feet point to point.
Height: Twelve feet, eight inches. See floor plan No. 5.
Knock—down Model

WOODROW

Size: Eight feet by twelve feet.
Height: Twelve feet, three inches. See floor plan No. 17.

Size: Thirteen feet point to point.
Height: Thirteen feet, nine inches. See floor plan No. 9.

GRANVILLE

Size: Thirteen feet point to point.
Height: Twelve feet, six inches. See floor plan No. 9.

Size: Nine feet, two inches point to point.
Height: Fifteen feet, six inches. See floor plan No. 1.

ARMITAGE

Size: Twelve feet by twelve feet.
Height: Eighteen feet, six inches. See floor plan No. 26.

Size: Twenty-one feet point to point.
Height: Twenty-one feet. See floor plan No. 12.

Size: Twenty-one feet point to point.
Height: Twenty feet. See floor plan No. 10.
MONTICELLO (same design)
Size: Twelve feet, point to point.
See floor plan No. 5.

WILLOWBROOK

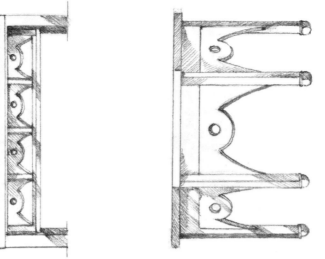

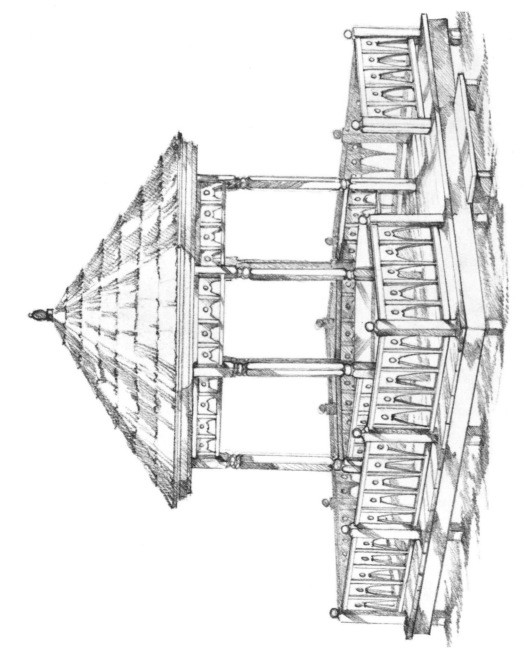

Size: Eighteen feet by eighteen feet.
Height: Fifteen feet, six inches. See floor plan No. 34.

VUE DES FLEURS

Size: Twelve feet point to point.
Height: Fourteen feet. See floor plan No. 5.

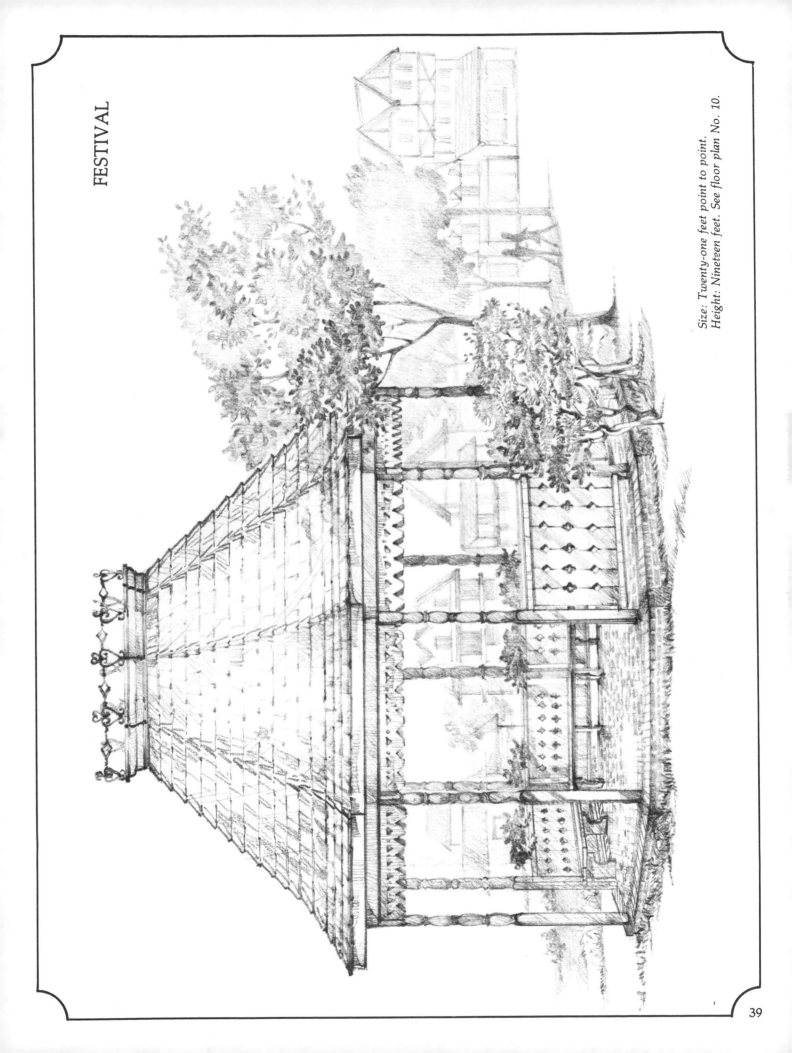

FESTIVAL

Size: Twenty-one feet point to point.
Height: Nineteen feet. See floor plan No. 10.

39

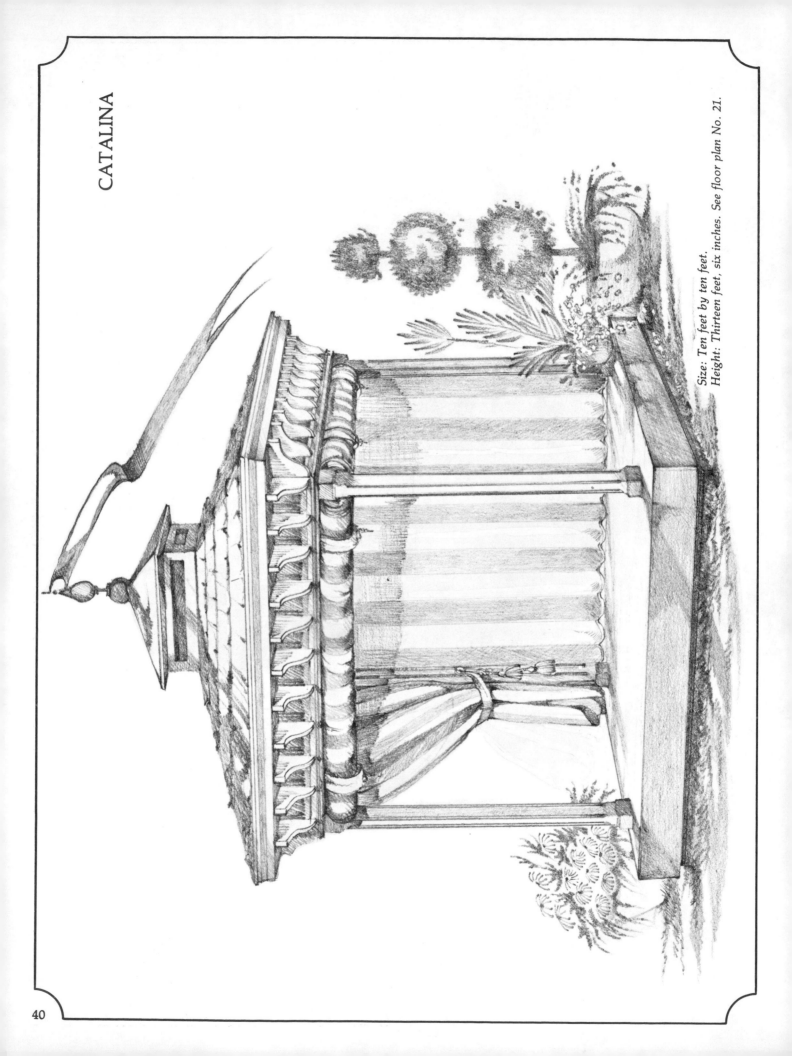

CATALINA

Size: Ten feet by ten feet.
Height: Thirteen feet, six inches. See floor plan No. 21.

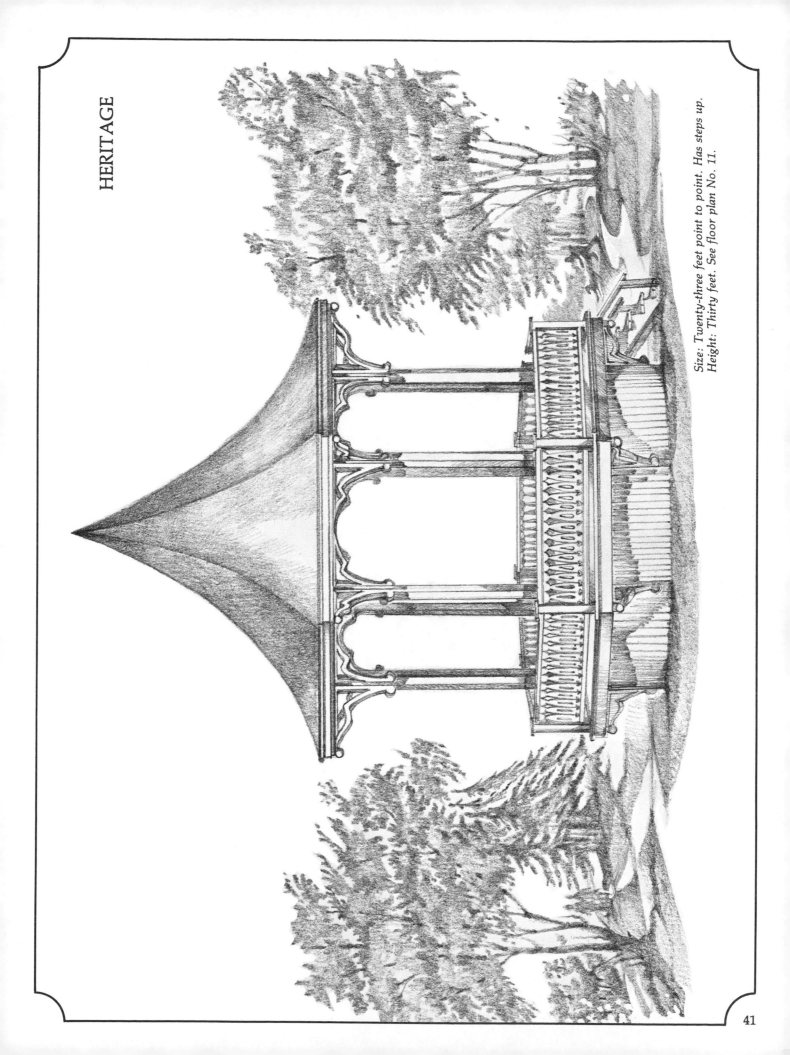

HERITAGE

Size: Twenty-three feet point to point. Has steps up.
Height: Thirty feet. See floor plan No. 11.

LEXINGTON

Size: Ten feet by ten feet.
Height: Eighteen feet. See floor plan No. 22.

42

SILVERLAKE

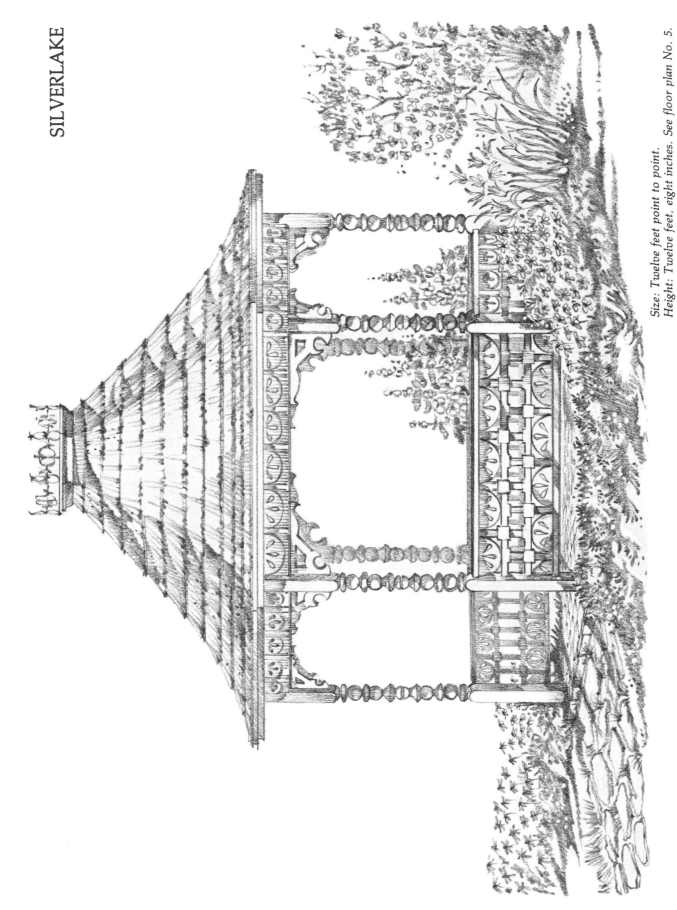

Size: Twelve feet point to point.
Height: Twelve feet, eight inches. See floor plan No. 5.

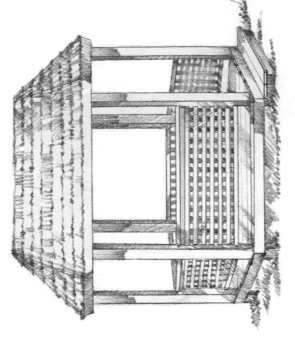

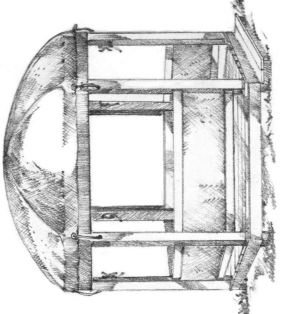

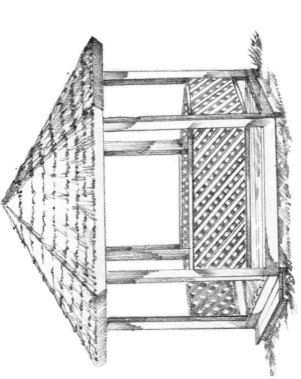

Size: Nine feet, two inches point to point.
Height: Varies with each plan. See floor plan No. 1.

CHESAPEAKE

Size: Twelve feet by eighteen feet.
Height: Nineteen feet, ten inches. See floor plan No. 28.

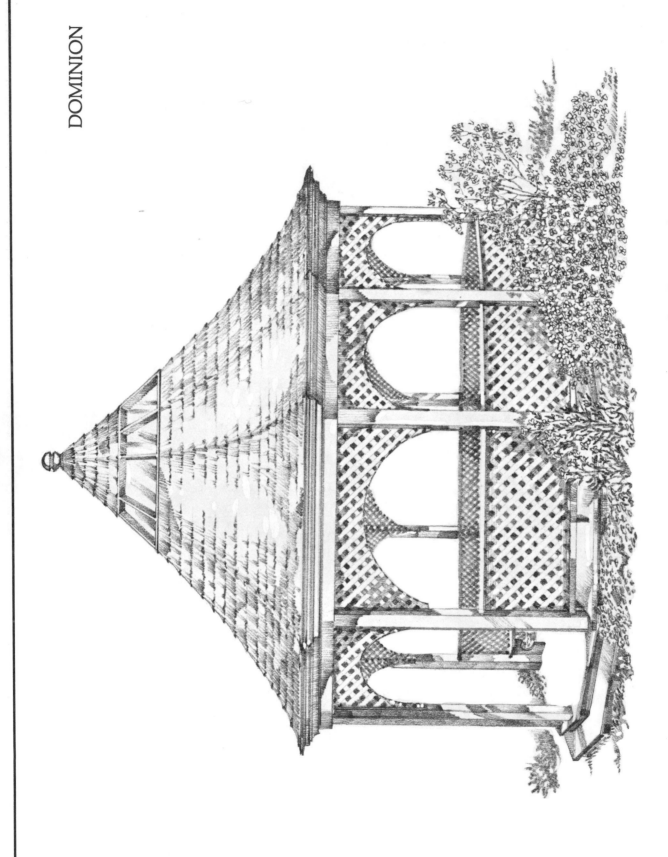

Size: Twenty-one feet point to point.
Height: Twenty feet, eight inches. See floor plan No. 10.

TIMBERLANE

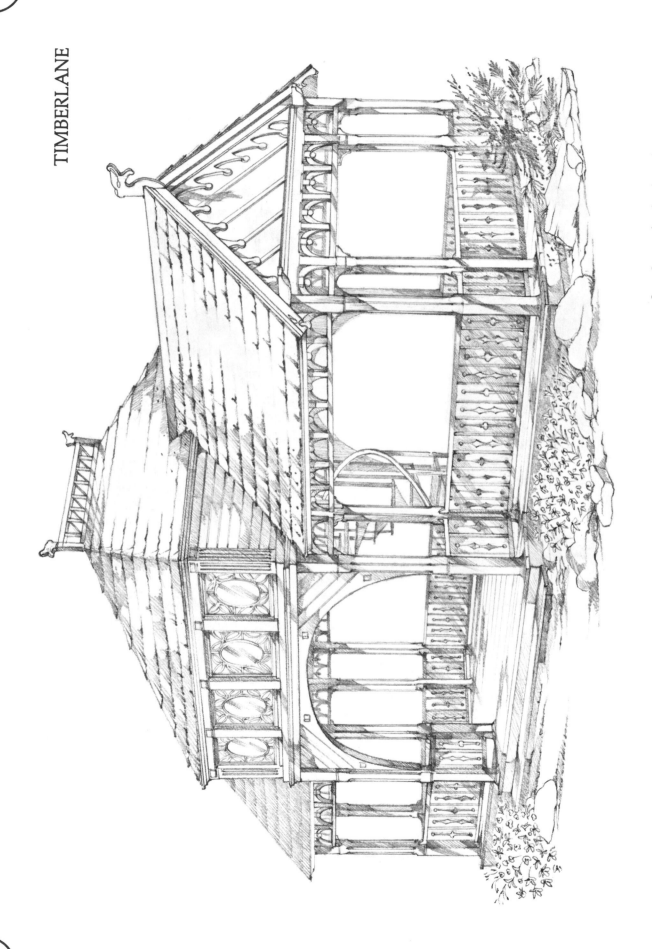

Size: Sixteen feet by thirty feet.
Height: Twenty-one feet. See floor plan No. 37.

WOODBRIDGE

Size: Six feet by six feet.
Height: Twelve feet, three inches. See floor plan No. 13.

SPRINGWATER

Size: Twelve feet, six inches by sixteen feet.
Height: Twenty feet, three inches. See floor plan No. 29.

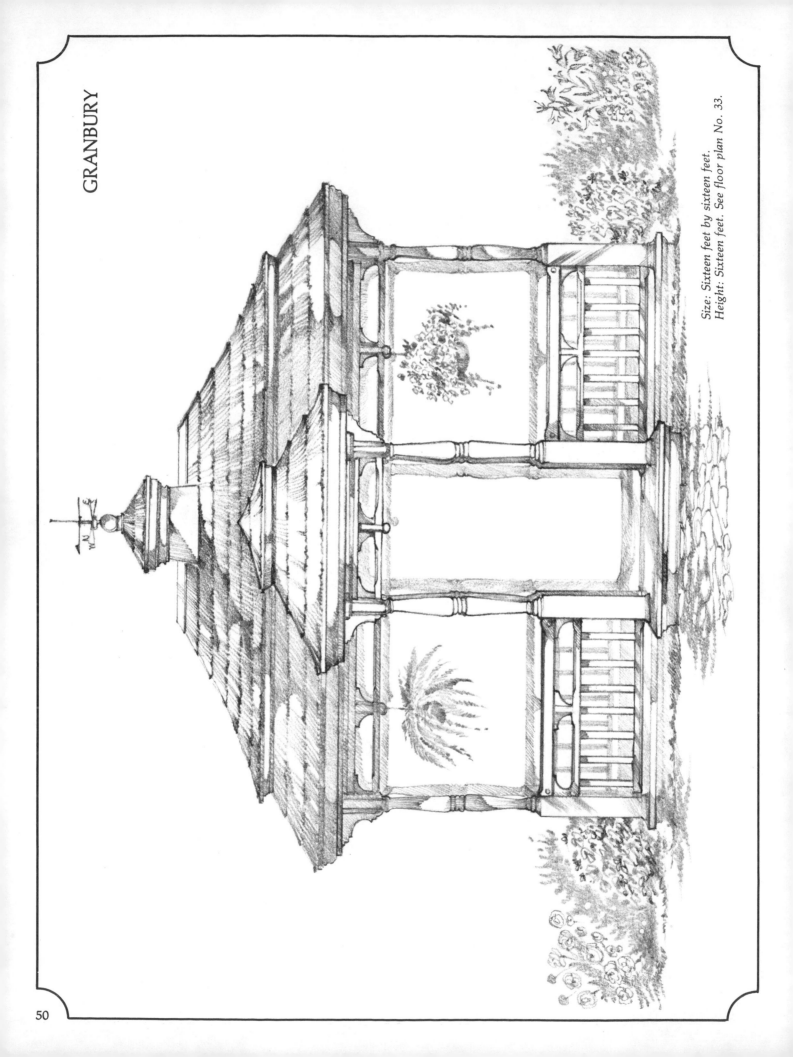

GRANBURY

Size: Sixteen feet by sixteen feet.
Height: Sixteen feet. See floor plan No. 33.

50

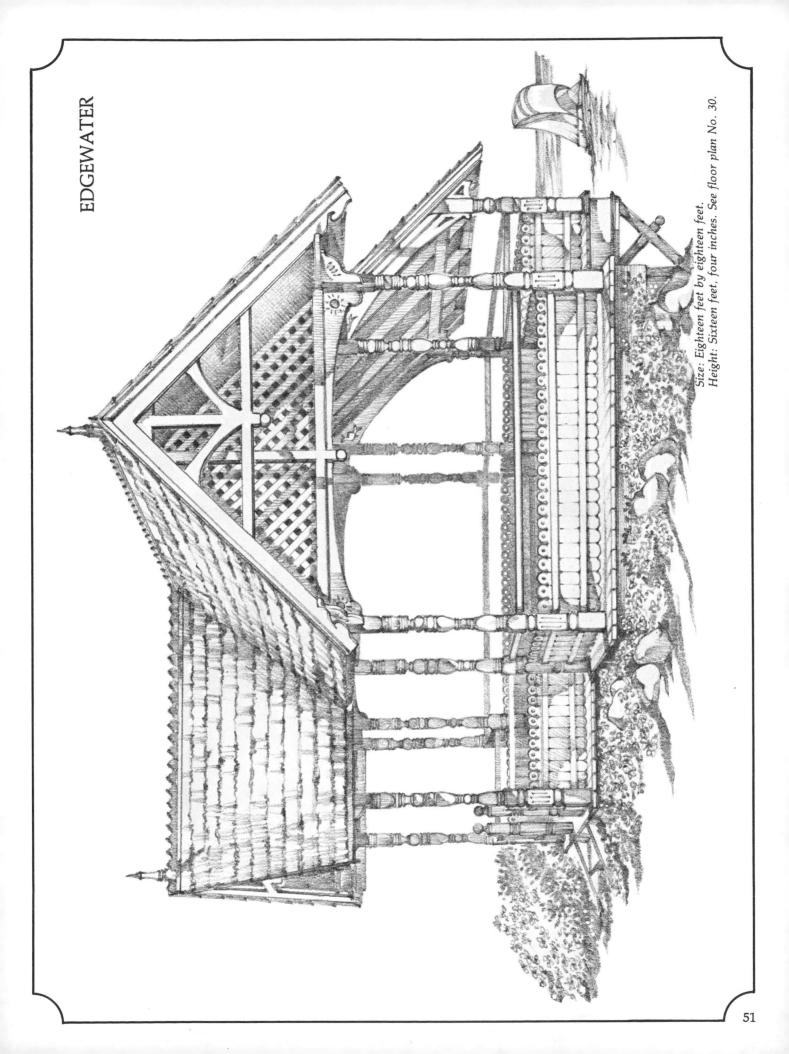

EDGEWATER

Size: Eighteen feet by eighteen feet.
Height: Sixteen feet, four inches. See floor plan No. 30.

Size: Twenty-one feet point to point.
Height: Twenty-four feet, six inches. See floor plan No. 10.

EMERALD

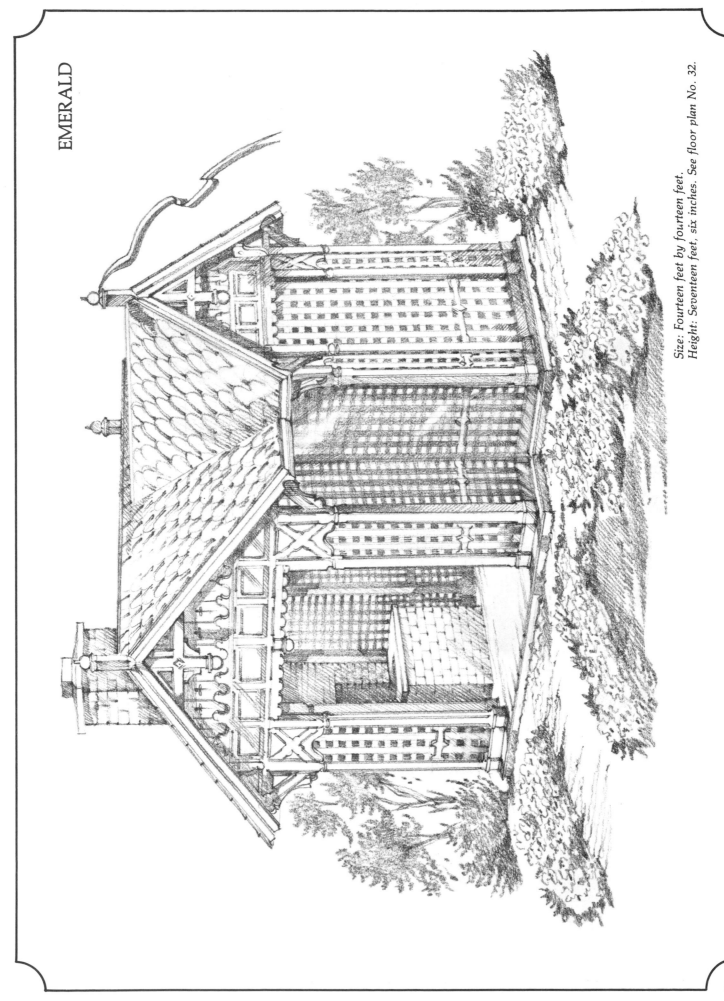

Size: Fourteen feet by fourteen feet.
Height: Seventeen feet, six inches. See floor plan No. 32.

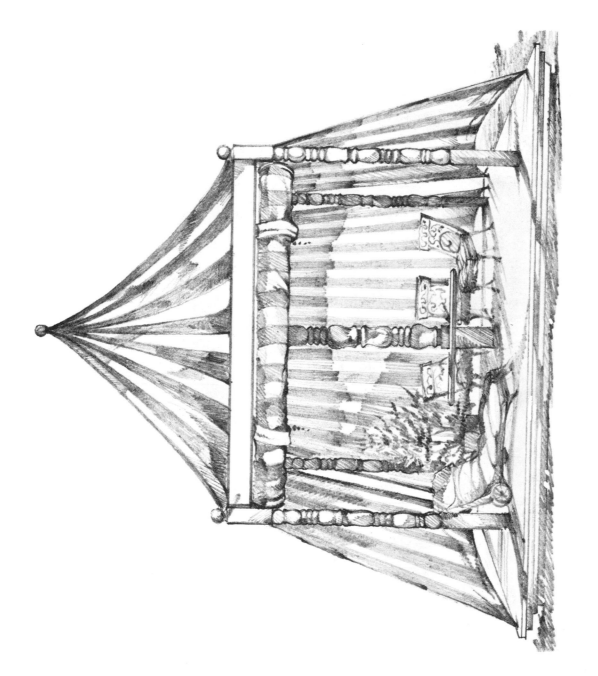

Size: Sixteen feet by sixteen feet.
Height: Fourteen feet. See floor plan No. 50.

SARATOGA

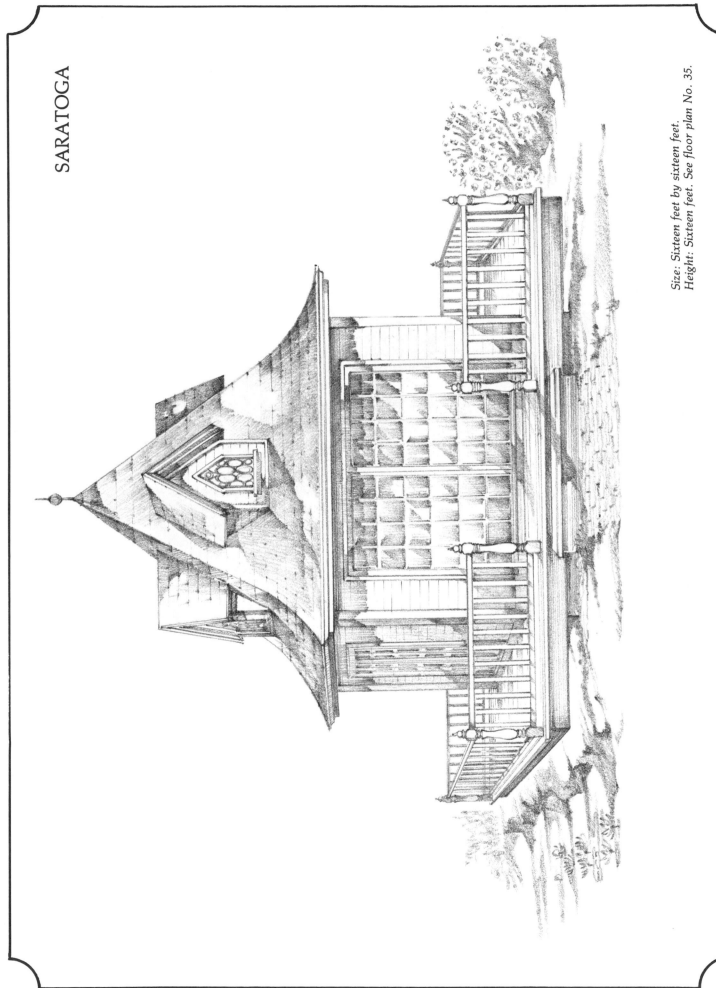

Size: Sixteen feet by sixteen feet.
Height: Sixteen feet. See floor plan No. 35.

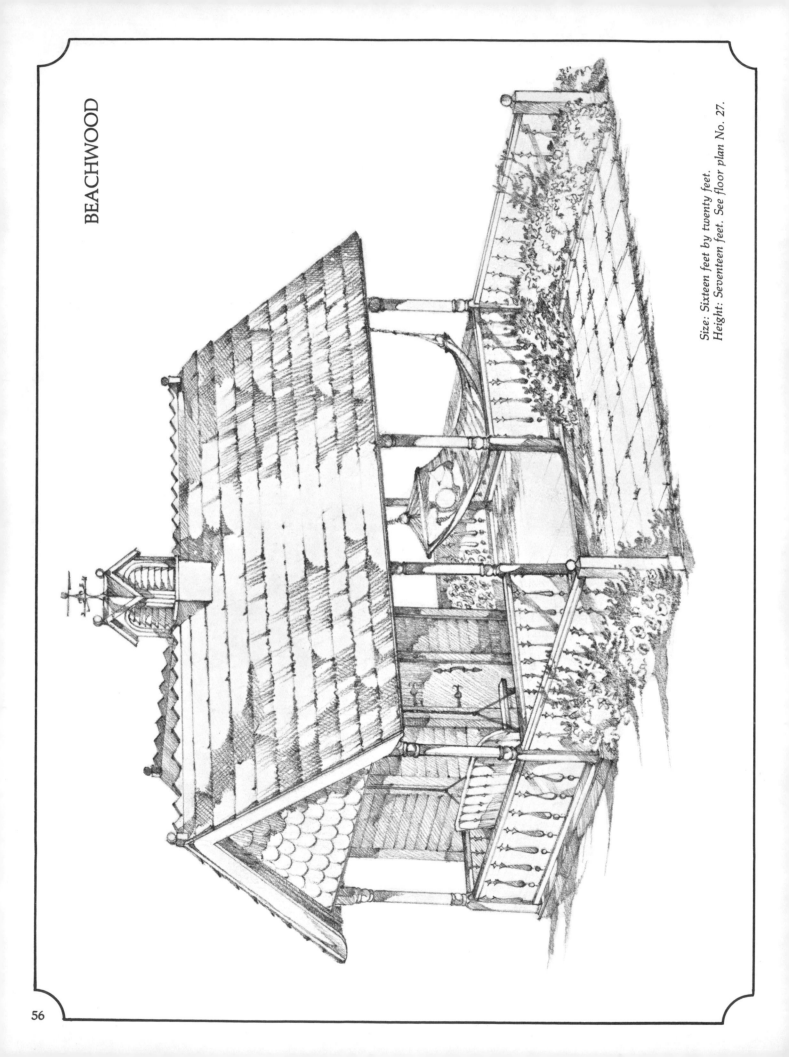

BEACHWOOD

Size: Sixteen feet by twenty feet.
Height: Seventeen feet. See floor plan No. 27.

BARONET

Size: Seventeen feet, eight inches point to point.
Height: Eleven feet, four inches.
See floor plan No. 7.

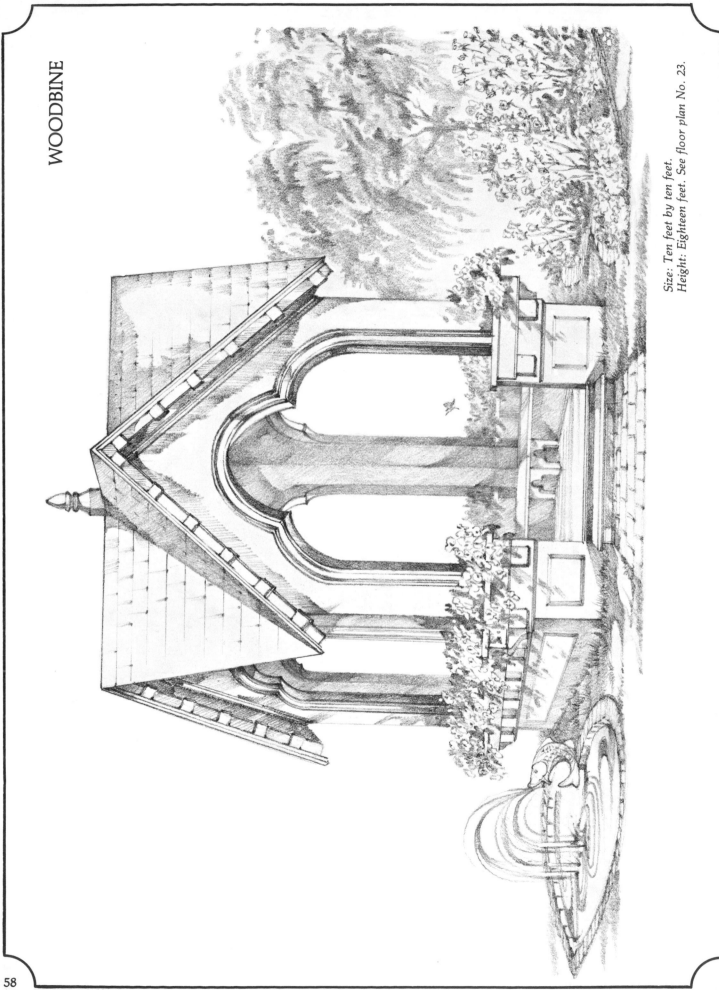

Size: Ten feet by ten feet.
Height: Eighteen feet. See floor plan No. 23.

THAXTON

Size: Ten feet by twelve feet.
Height: Seventeen feet. See floor plan No. 24.

ARBORS

SHILOH

Size: Nine feet, four inches by six feet.
Height: Eleven feet, three inches. See floor plan No. 53.

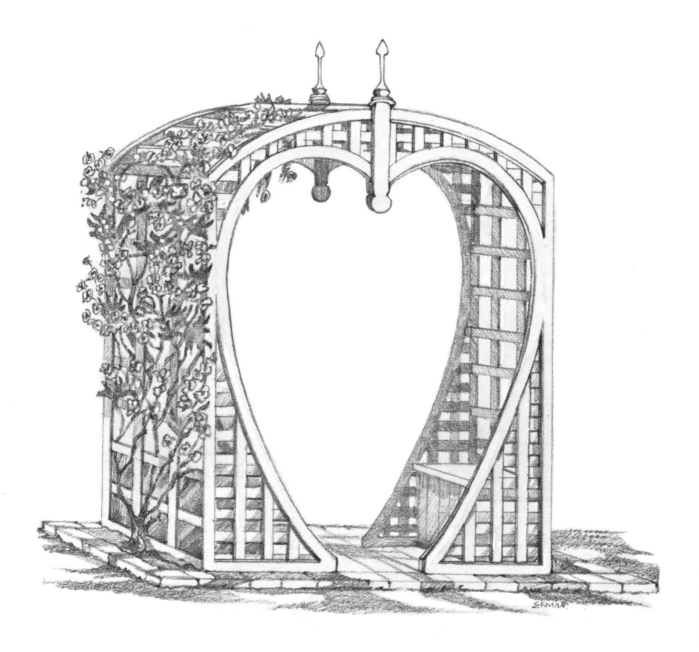

Size: Seven feet by four feet.
Height: Nine feet. See floor plan No. 54.

GREENWOOD

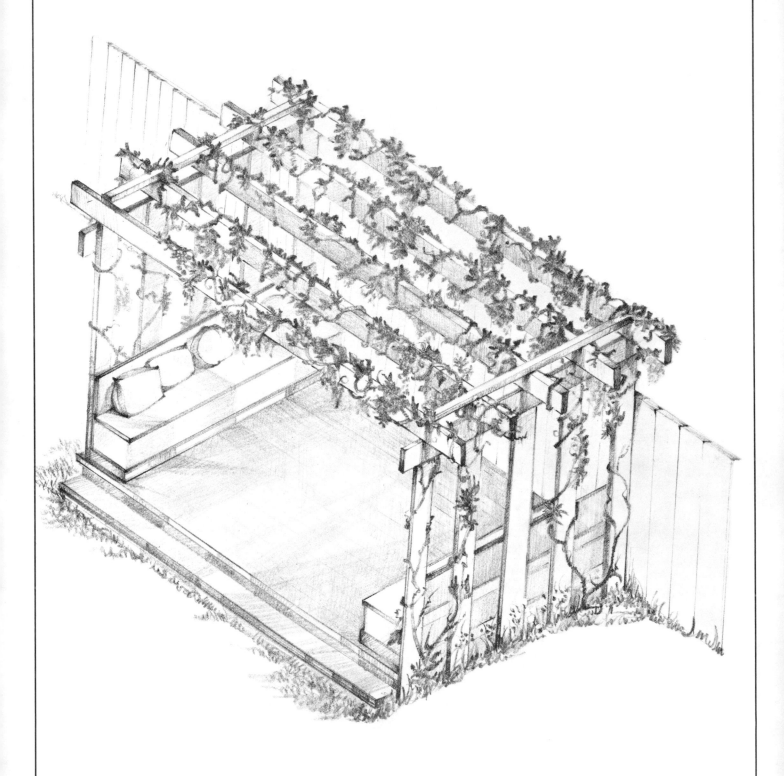

Size: Twelve feet by ten feet.
Height: Nine feet. See floor plan No. 51.

Size: Nine feet, four inches by seven feet, four inches.
Height: Eight feet, six inches. See floor plan No. 52.

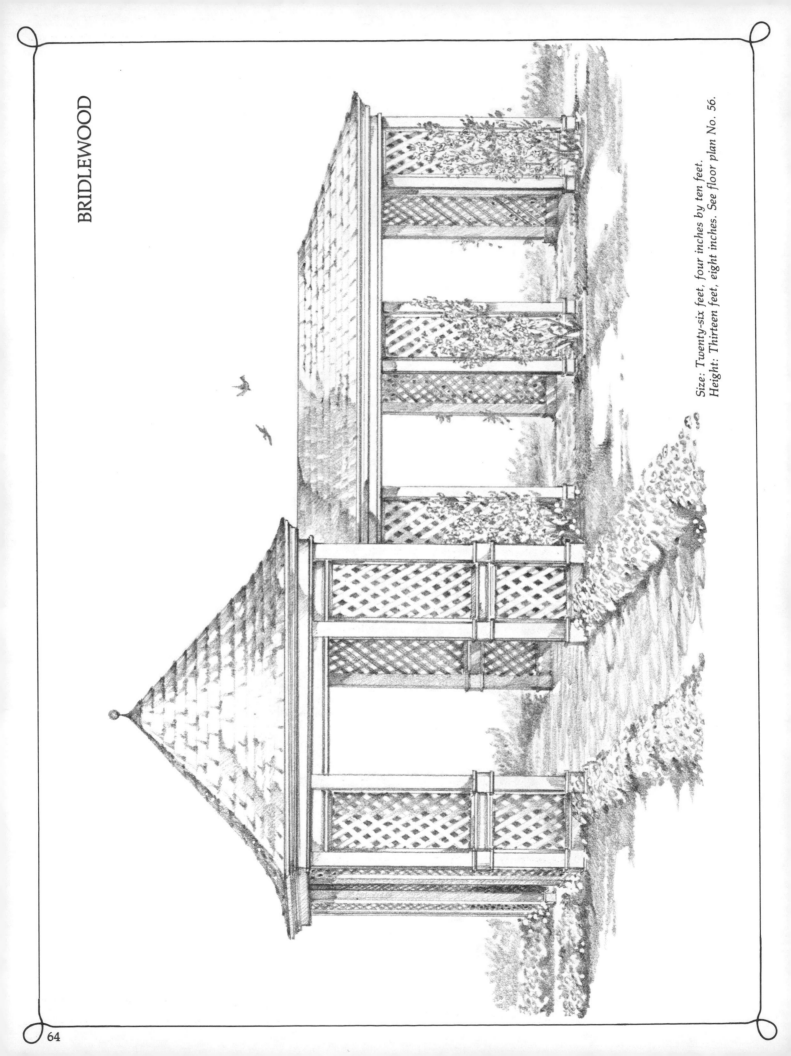

BRIDLEWOOD

Size: Twenty-six feet, four inches by ten feet.
Height: Thirteen feet, eight inches. See floor plan No. 56.

OLD HICKORY

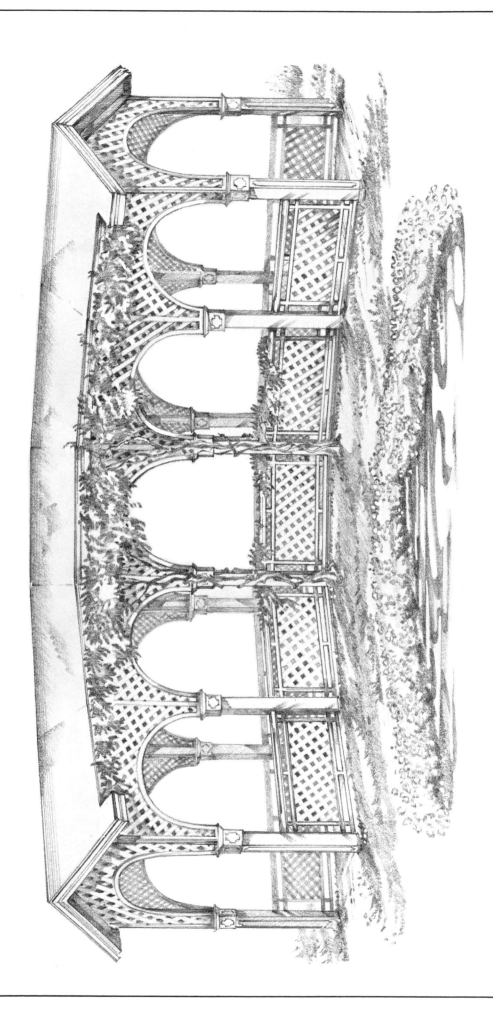

Size: Eight feet, eight inches by thirty feet, three inches.
Height: Twelve feet, six inches. See floor plan No. 57.

ALDERLY

Size: Fourteen feet by fourteen feet.
Height: Nine feet, eight inches. See floor plan No. 55.

STROMBRELLAS

FAIRFAX

Size: Three feet, six inches by five feet, eight inches.
Height: Eight feet, two inches. See floor plan No. 42.

PARKWOOD

Size: Eight feet by eight feet.
Height: Eight feet, four inches. See floor plan No. 48.

Size: Eight feet, nine inches by five feet.
Height: Ten feet, three inches. See floor plan No. 38.

BERKELEY

Size: Seven feet, eight inches by four feet, eight inches.
Height: Nine feet, five inches. See floor plan No. 47.

Size: Six feet by four feet.
Height: Eight feet. See floor plan No. 40.

CHESTERTON

Size: Four feet by four feet.
Height: Seven feet, six inches. See floor plan No. 41.

Size: Twelve feet by eight feet.
Height: Sixteen feet, five inches. See floor plan No. 49.

BRIGHTON

Size: Seven feet, eight inches by four feet, eight inches.
Height: Nine feet, five inches. See floor plan No. 47.

Size: Seven feet by seven feet.
Height: Nine feet, eight inches. See floor plan No. 43.

PROVIDENCE

Ekman

Size: Five feet, four inches by five feet, four inches.
Height: Ten feet, three inches. See floor plan No. 39.

Size: Seven feet by seven feet.
Height: Fifteen feet. See floor plan No. 44.

PENDLETON

Size: Twelve feet by three feet, six inches.
Height: Twelve feet, six inches. See floor plan No. 46.

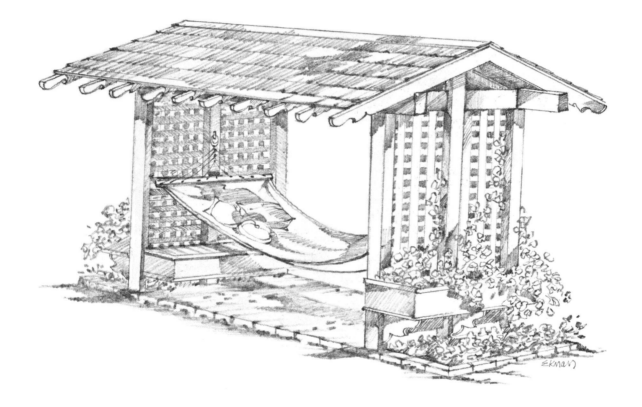

Size: Eleven feet, ten inches by five feet, six inches
Height: Eight feet. See floor plan No. 45.

BIRDFEEDERS & BIRDHOUSES

MOURNING DOVE

Size: Eleven inches by eleven inches.
Height: Fourteen inches. Feeder.

SPARROW

Size: Twenty-one inches by twenty-one inches.
Height: Thirty-two inches. House.

GOLDFINCH

Size: Twelve inches by twenty-four inches.
Height: Eighteen inches. Feeder.

BLUEBIRD

Size: Ten inches by ten inches.
Height: Eleven inches. Feeder, with glass.

WREN

Size: Eight inches by eight inches.
Height: Ten inches. House.

BUNTING

Size: Fourteen inches by fourteen inches.
Height: Thirteen inches. Feeder.

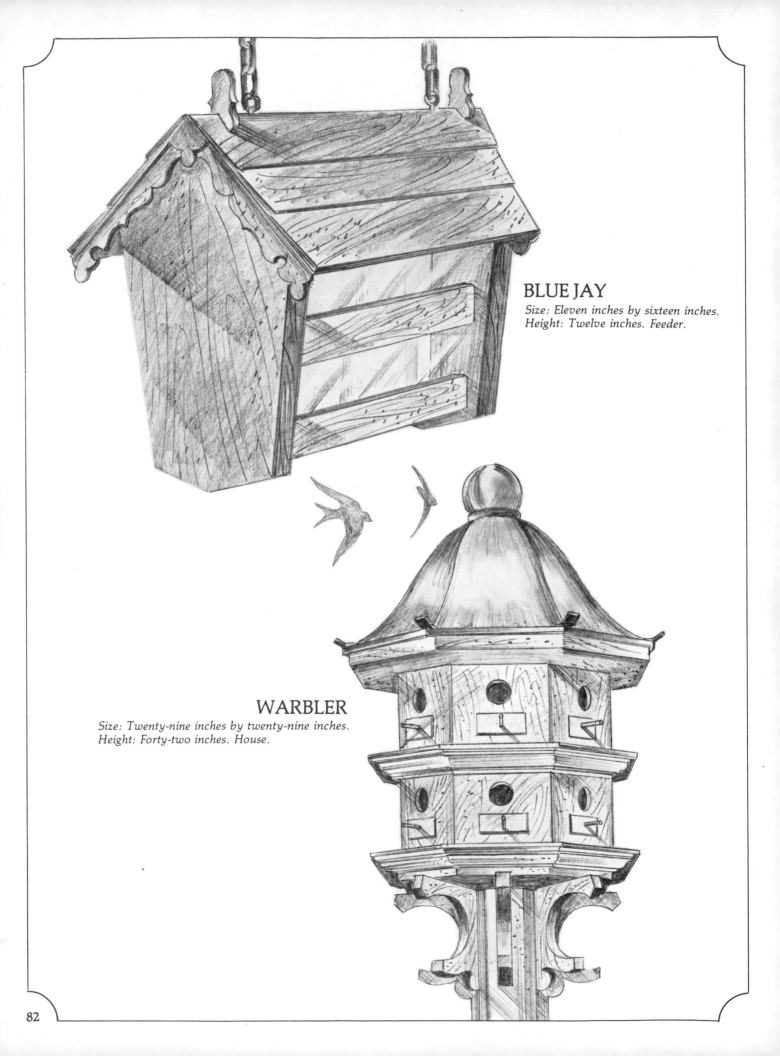

BLUE JAY

Size: Eleven inches by sixteen inches.
Height: Twelve inches. Feeder.

WARBLER

Size: Twenty-nine inches by twenty-nine inches.
Height: Forty-two inches. House.

WOODPECKER
Size: Thirteen inches by sixteen inches.
Height: Twelve inches. Feeder, with glass.

THRASHER
Size: Twenty-six inches by twenty-six inches.
Height: Forty-two inches. Feeder, with glass.

NUTHATCH
Size: Thirteen inches by thirteen inches.
Height: Thirteen inches. Feeder, with glass.

THRUSH

Size: Eighteen inches by eighteen inches.
Height: Twenty inches. Feeder, with glass.

ORIOLE

Size: Fourteen inches by fourteen inches.
Height: Fourteen inches. Feeder, with glass.

CHICKADEE

Size: Nine and a half inches by eight and a half inches.
Height: Seven and a half inches. Feeder.

SWALLOW

Size: Twenty-seven inches and twenty-seven inches.
Height: Forty-eight inches. House.

CARDINAL

Size: Fourteen inches by ten and one-quarter inches.
Height: Eight and a half inches. Feeder, with glass.

TWO BIRDFEEDER PLANS

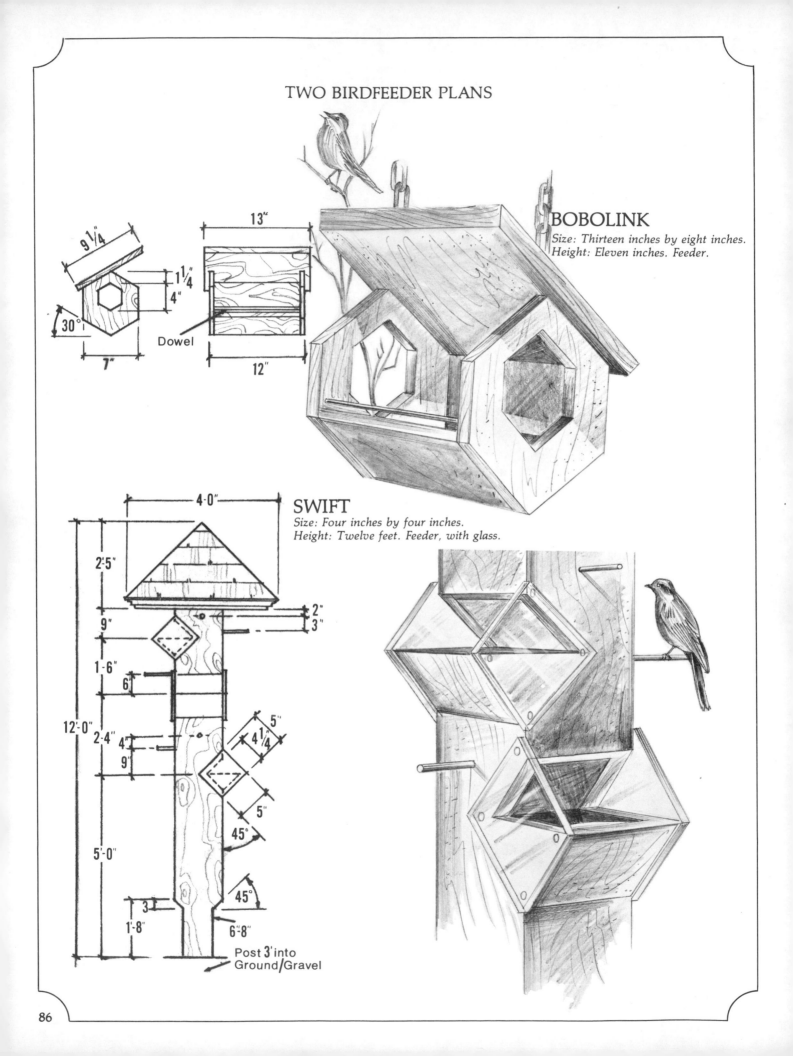

BOBOLINK
Size: Thirteen inches by eight inches.
Height: Eleven inches. Feeder.

9 1/4"

13"

1 1/4"

4"

30°

7"

Dowel

12"

SWIFT
Size: Four inches by four inches.
Height: Twelve feet. Feeder, with glass.

4'-0"

2'-5"

9"

2"

3"

1'-6"

6"

12'-0"

2'-4"

4"

9"

5"

4 1/4"

5"

45°

45°

5'-0"

3"

1'-8"

6"-8"

Post 3' into
Ground/Gravel

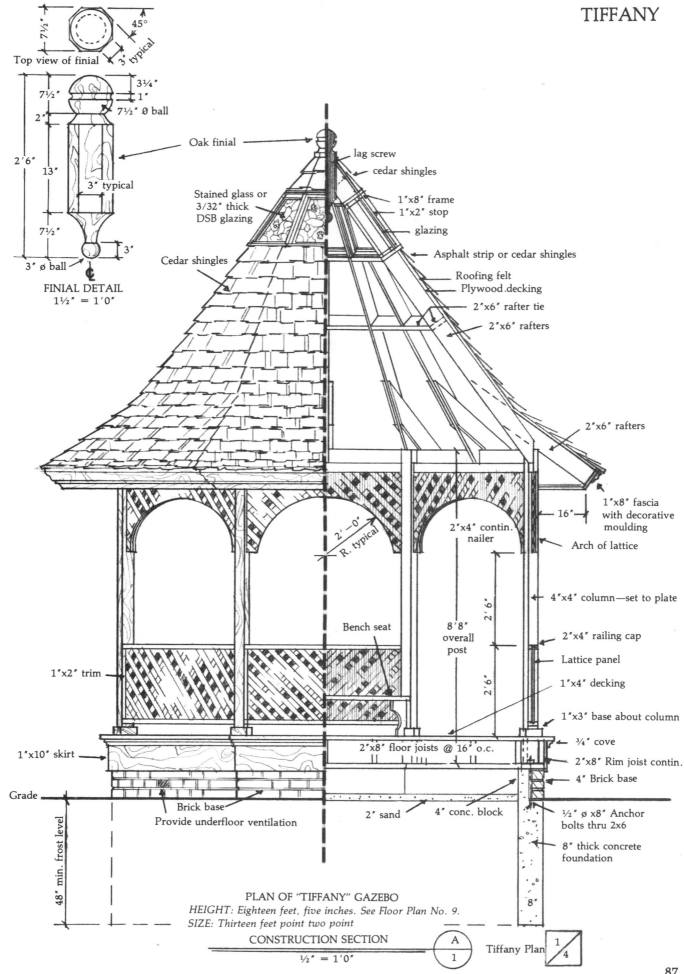

Top view of finial

7½″ 45° 3″ typical

Oak finial

3¼″
1″
7½″ ∅ ball
7½″
2″
13″
3″ typical
2′6″
7½″
3″
3″ ∅ ball

FINIAL DETAIL
1½″ = 1′0″

lag screw
cedar shingles
1″x8″ frame
1″x2″ stop
glazing

Stained glass or
3/32″ thick
DSB glazing

Asphalt strip or cedar shingles
Roofing felt
Plywood.decking
2″x6″ rafter tie
2″x6″ rafters

Cedar shingles

2″x6″ rafters

1″x8″ fascia
with decorative
moulding
16″

Arch of lattice

2′—0″
R. typical

2″x4″ contin.
nailer

4″x4″ column—set to plate

Bench seat

8′8″
overall
post

2′6″

2′6″

2″x4″ railing cap

Lattice panel

1″x4″ decking

1″x3″ base about column

¾″ cove

1″x2″ trim

1″x10″ skirt

2″x8″ floor joists @ 16″ o.c.

2″x8″ Rim joist contin.

4″ Brick base

Grade

Brick base
Provide underfloor ventilation

2″ sand   4″ conc. block

½″ ∅ x8″ Anchor
bolts thru 2x6

8″ thick concrete
foundation

48″ min. frost level

8″

PLAN OF "TIFFANY" GAZEBO
HEIGHT: Eighteen feet, five inches. See Floor Plan No. 9.
SIZE: Thirteen feet point two point

CONSTRUCTION SECTION   A
—————————————————   1   Tiffany Plan   1/4
½″ = 1′0″

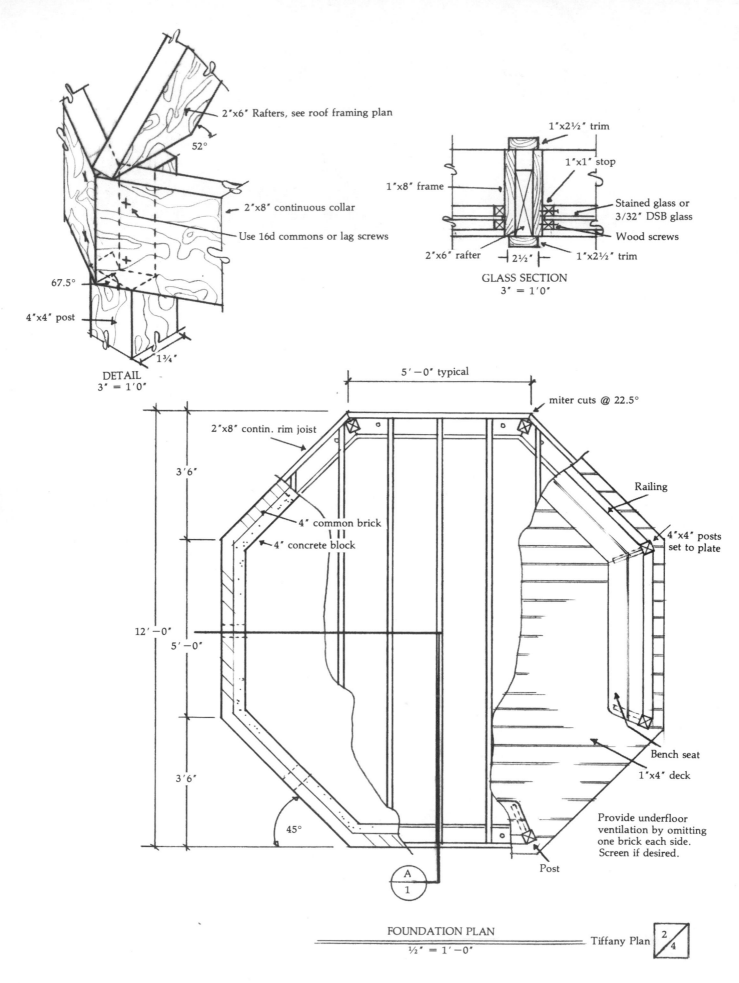

2"x6" Rafters, see roof framing plan

52°

2"x8" continuous collar

Use 16d commons or lag screws

67.5°

4"x4" post

1¾"

DETAIL
3" = 1'0"

1"x2½" trim

1"x8" frame

1"x1" stop

Stained glass or
3/32" DSB glass

Wood screws

2"x6" rafter

2½"

1"x2½" trim

GLASS SECTION
3" = 1'0"

5'−0" typical

miter cuts @ 22.5°

2"x8" contin. rim joist

3'6"

Railing

4'x4' posts
set to plate

4" common brick

4" concrete block

12'−0"

5'−0"

Bench seat

1"x4" deck

3'6"

45°

Provide underfloor
ventilation by omitting
one brick each side.
Screen if desired.

Post

A
1

FOUNDATION PLAN

½" = 1'−0"

Tiffany Plan

2
4

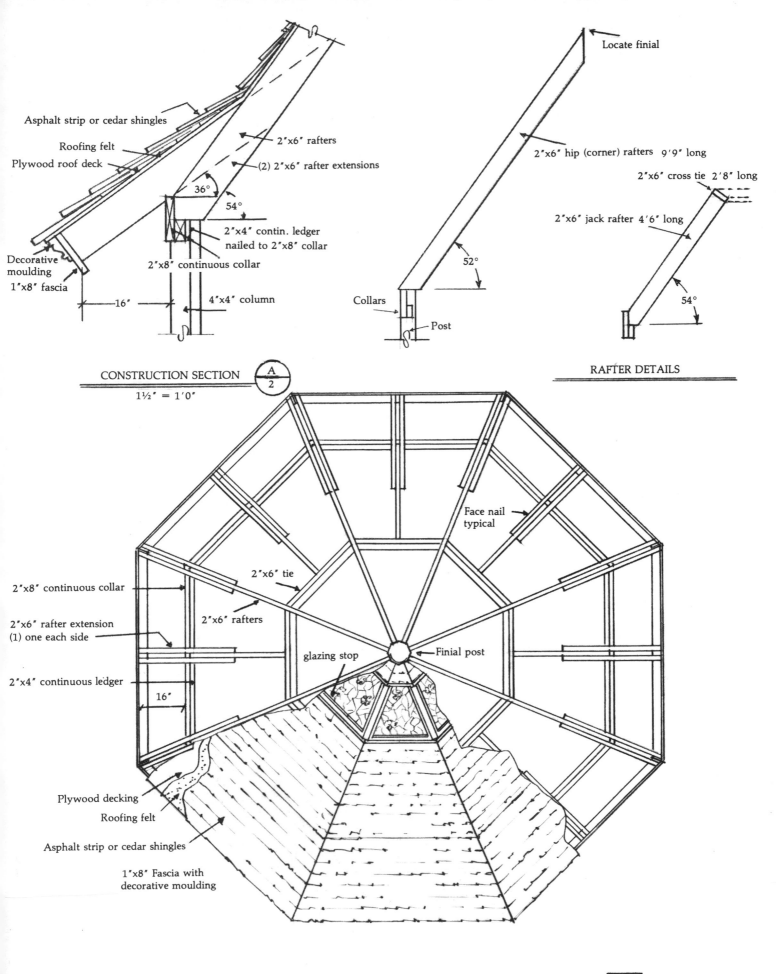

Asphalt strip or cedar shingles

Roofing felt

Plywood roof deck

2"x6" rafters

(2) 2"x6" rafter extensions

36°

54°

2"x4" contin. ledger nailed to 2"x8" collar

2"x8" continuous collar

Decorative moulding

1"x8" fascia

16"

4"x4" column

CONSTRUCTION SECTION A/2

1½" = 1'0"

Locate finial

2"x6" hip (corner) rafters 9'9" long

2"x6" cross tie 2'8" long

2"x6" jack rafter 4'6" long

52°

54°

Collars

Post

RAFTER DETAILS

Face nail typical

2"x8" continuous collar

2"x6" tie

2"x6" rafter extension (1) one each side

2"x6" rafters

2"x4" continuous ledger

16"

glazing stop

Finial post

Plywood decking

Roofing felt

Asphalt strip or cedar shingles

1"x8" Fascia with decorative moulding

ROOF FRAMING PLAN

½" = 1' – 0"

Tiffany Plan 3/4

89

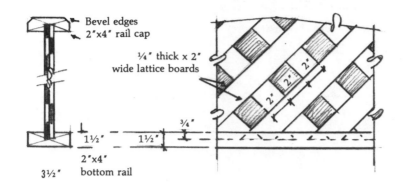

RAILING DETAILS

$3'' = 1'0''$

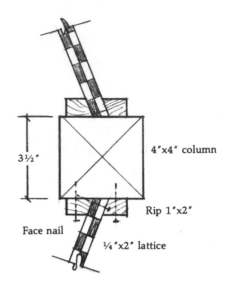

POST DETAIL

$3'' = 1'0''$

MATERIAL LIST

Item #	Description	Quantity
1.	Concrete (Foundation) 3000 PSI	4 CY
2.	4″ Concrete Block	32 EA
3.	Common Brick (veneer base)	200 EA
4.	½″ø x 8″ Anchor Bolts	16 EA
5.	2″x6″ Pressure treated fir (Plate)	40 LF
6.	2″x8″ Douglas Fir (Floor joists & bridging)	98 LF
7.	1″x10″ Clear Pine (Skirt)	40 LF
8.	Cove Moulding (Skirt trim)	40 LF
9.	1″x4″ T&G Decking—Douglas Fir	390 LF
10.	4″x4″ Columns—Fir—8′8″ long	8 EA
11.	1″x3″ Pine (Column base trim)	12 LF
12.	2″x4″ s4s Douglas Fir (Rail cap & bottom)	60 LF
13.	2″x4″ s4s Douglas Fir (Ledger)	40 LF
14.	2″x8″ s4s Douglas Fir (Collar)	40 LF
15.	2″x6″ s4s Douglas Fir (Rafters)	276 LF
16.	1″x1″ Pine (Stop @ glazing)	56 LF
17.	1″x8″ Pine (Glazing frame)	56 LF
18.	Alternate roof deckings:	
	1″x4″ Pine (Sleepers)	400 LF
	1″x6″ T&G Fir with 15# felt over	800 LF
	½″ CDX Plywood with 15# felt over	11 SHTS
19.	Cedar Shingles and felt—288 SF=2.8 Sq.	2.8 SQ. EA
20.	¼″x2″ Pine (Lattice boards)	800 LF
21.	1″x8″ Clear Pine (Fascia board)	53 LF
22.	Picture Moulding (Fascia trim)	53 LF
23.	1″x2½″ Clear Pine Trim (@ glazing)	64 LF
24.	8″x8″ Douglas Fir Turned Finial	1 EA
25.	Stained Glass Panels (Design by Owner)	8 EA
26.	¼″x6″ Lag Screws (Anchor rafters to finial)	8 EA
27.	2″x12″ Fir (Bench seat support)	12 LF
28.	2″x6″ s4s Pine (Seat boards)	28 LF
29.	2″x8″ s4s Pine (Seat boards)	27 LF
30.	Teco Clips (Rafters to collar)	16 EA
31.	Metal "L" Clips (Bench seat to deck)	16 EA
32.	Common Wire Nails as Required	

Construction plans may be ordered—
see complete price list on back cover

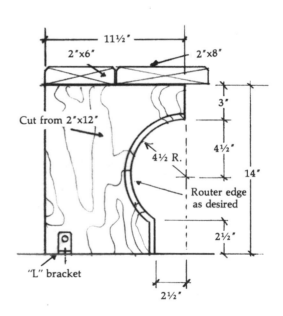

BENCH SEAT DETAIL

$1½'' - 1'0''$

Tiffany Plan

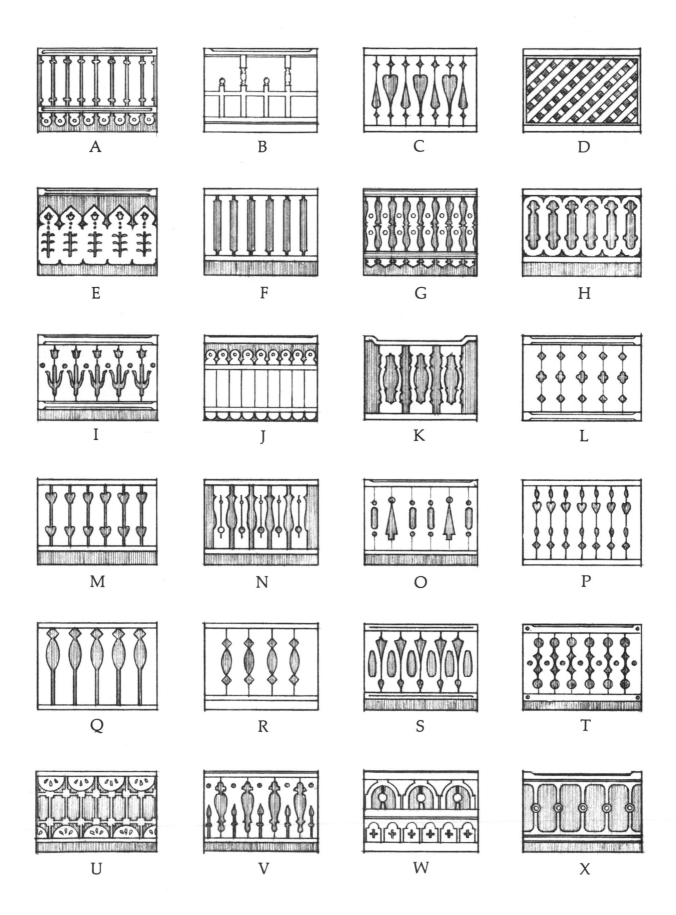

A

B

C

D

E

F

G

H

I

J

K

L

M

N

O

P

Q

R

S

T

U

V

W

X

CORNICE/FASCIA

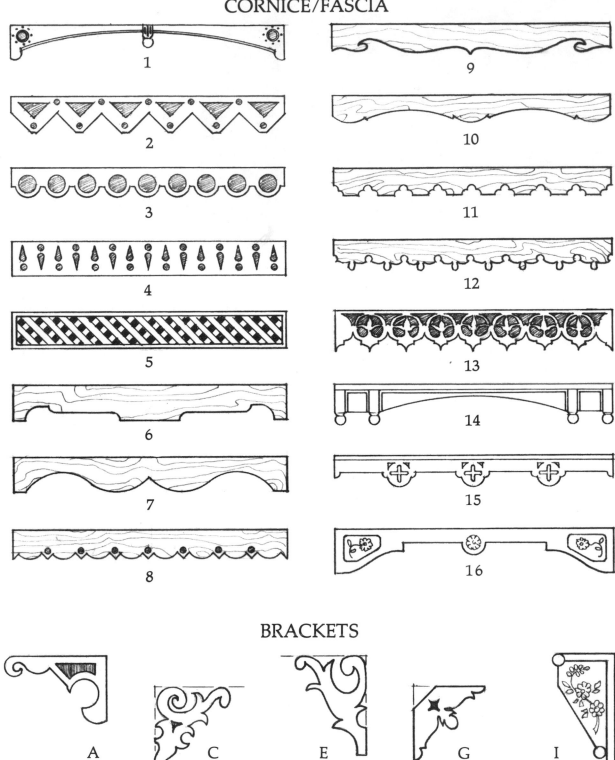

1

2

3

4

5

6

7

8

9

10

11

12

13

14

15

16

BRACKETS

A

B

C

D

E

F

G

H

I

J

FLOOR PLANS

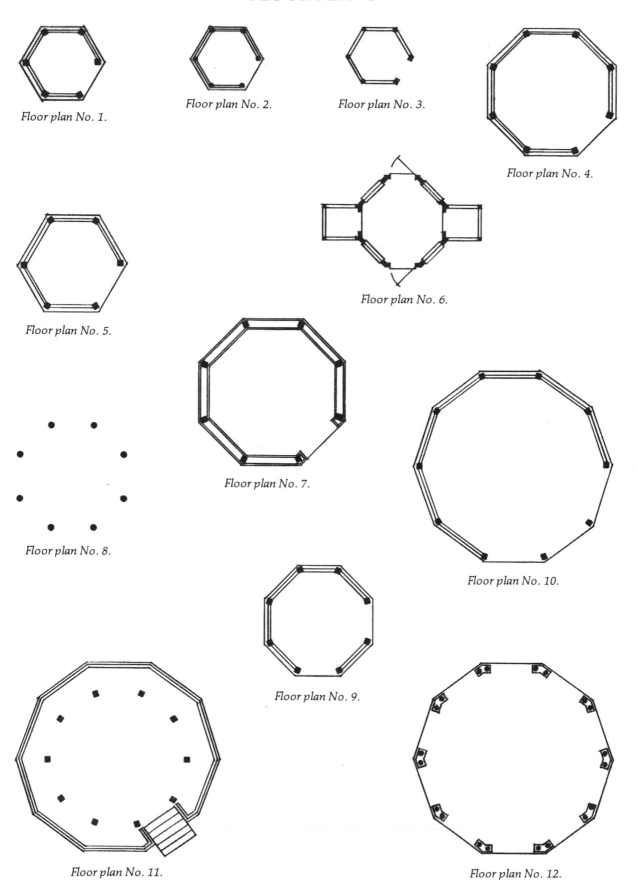

Floor plan No. 1.

Floor plan No. 2.

Floor plan No. 3.

Floor plan No. 4.

Floor plan No. 5.

Floor plan No. 6.

Floor plan No. 7.

Floor plan No. 8.

Floor plan No. 9.

Floor plan No. 10.

Floor plan No. 11.

Floor plan No. 12.

FLOOR PLANS

Floor plan No. 13.

Floor plan No. 14.

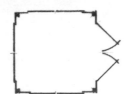

Floor plan No. 15.

Floor plan No. 16.

Floor plan No. 17.

Floor plan No. 18.

Floor plan No. 19.

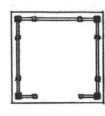

Floor plan No. 20.

Floor plan No. 21.

Floor plan No. 22.

Floor plan No. 23.

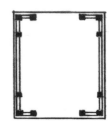

Floor plan No. 24.

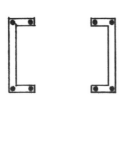

Floor plan No. 25.

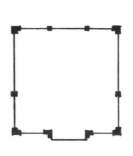

Floor plan No. 26.

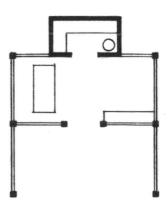

Floor plan No. 27.

FLOOR PLANS

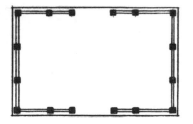

Floor plan No. 28.

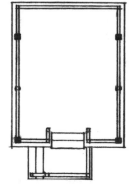

Floor plan No. 29.

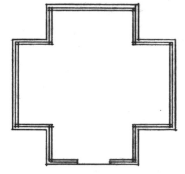

Floor plan No. 30.

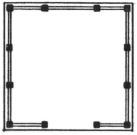

Floor plan No. 31.

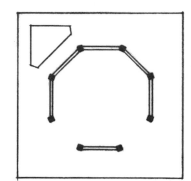

Floor plan No. 34.

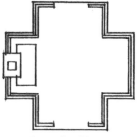

Floor plan No. 32.

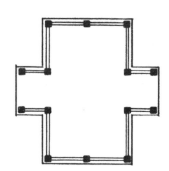

Floor plan No. 33.

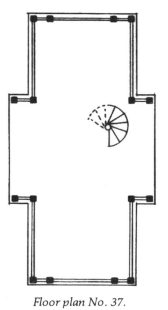

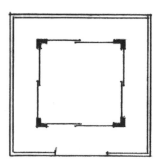

Floor plan No. 35.

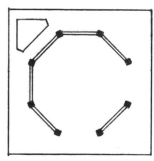

Floor plan No. 36.

Floor plan No. 37.

FLOOR PLANS

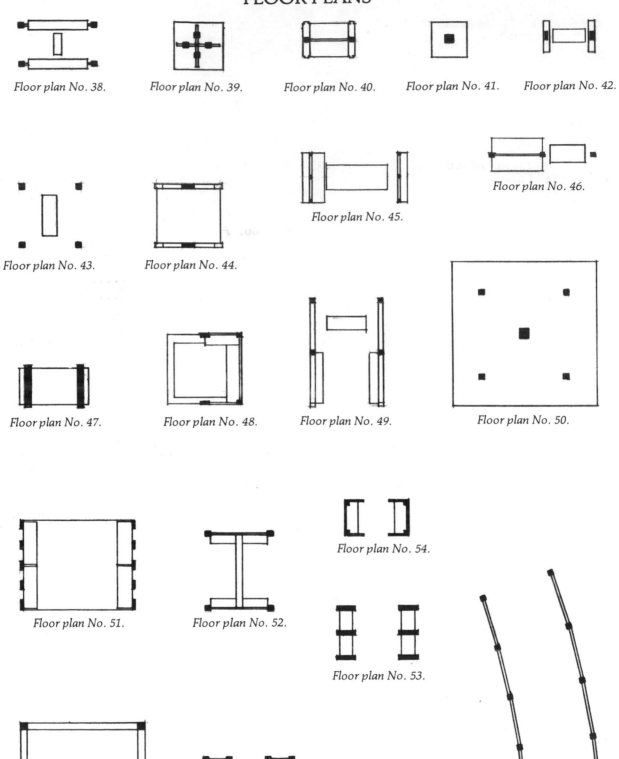

Floor plan No. 38.

Floor plan No. 39.

Floor plan No. 40.

Floor plan No. 41.

Floor plan No. 42.

Floor plan No. 43.

Floor plan No. 44.

Floor plan No. 45.

Floor plan No. 46.

Floor plan No. 47.

Floor plan No. 48.

Floor plan No. 49.

Floor plan No. 50.

Floor plan No. 51.

Floor plan No. 52.

Floor plan No. 53.

Floor plan No. 54.

Floor plan No. 55.

Floor plan No. 56.

Floor plan No. 57.